TEENAGE MOUTH

TEENAGE MOUTH

Roger Karshner

Dramaline Publications

Dramaline Publications
36-851 Palm View Road, Rancho Mirage, CA 92270
Phone 619/770-6076 Fax 619/770-4507
Email: drama.line@gte.net
Web: dramaline.com

Cover by Rod Dyer Group

This book is printed on paper meeting the requirements of the American National Standard of Permanence of paper for printed library material.

CONTENTS

YOUNG WOMEN

FELICIA

Felicia, shaken, tells of the gang-related slaying of a friend.

Last Saturday, Maria and I went to this party on 5th Street, okay? We hung out at the party for a couple of hours, dancing and having fun and talking to friends. Maria was a good dancer and was real popular. Everybody liked her.

We left the party around ten o'clock or so and started walking back home. After we'd walked about four blocks, this car pulls up and this guy yells out the window. He says, "Hey, we're from the North Side Gang and we're looking for some dude."

I didn't like the looks of these guys, and I told Maria that we should be careful and just keep on walking and not answer them. In this neighborhood, on the streets at night, you never know what's going to happen.

But Maria walks up to the car. She was always like that. She was never afraid or suspicious of people. So she walks up to the car and says, "I don't know you guys. If you were from the north side, I'd know you guys." Then this guy in the back of the car says, "We're from the south side, bitch." Then he pulls up this shotgun and shoots Maria in the arm. It was terrible.

Maria fell down on her knees holding her arm. It looked like her arm was almost torn off from the shotgun and blood was shooting out all over the place. I ran into a yard and up on the front porch of this house. The guys in the car called Maria a slut and laughed at her. I knew she was hurt real bad, but there wasn't anything I could do but try to keep them from shooting me, too. Gang guys don't care who they kill.

Maria was crying and holding her arm and begging them not to hurt her. She said, "Please, I didn't do anything. Don't hurt me, please."

Then the guy with the shotgun shot her again and she fell back. I heard her call out for her mother. "Mother," she said. "Oh, Mother!" Then she kind of like trembled and died. I still can see it. It was . . . it was awful. I can still see it. I'll never get it out of my mind. Ever.

Maria didn't do anything. All she wanted was to have a life. And now here she is, dead at sixteen.

In this neighborhood, on the streets at night, you never know what's going to happen.

SHIRLEY

Shirley can think of nothing worse than vacationing with her family.

So I tell Mom, I say, "Look, Mom, I'd rather eat a live snake than hang out for two whole weeks with you and Dad and Norman in the middle of some wilderness in Idaho somewhere. Besides, I can't take Norman. I don't care if he's my little brother or not, he's a dork. He's built like this little tank and he's just as destructive. Why can't I stay home? I'm too old for family vacations."

And she says, "You'll have to talk to your father about that." They always cop out like this when they haven't got nerve enough to be honest, to give you bad news themselves. If I would have asked Dad, he would have said, "You'll have to talk to your mother about that." You ever notice how they do that? Pass the buck? A neat trick, huh? So much for parents.

So I go and talk to Dad and tell him that the thought of spending two weeks in the back of our van with Norman makes me puke. Besides, who needs Idaho? Like what the hell does Idaho have to offer, anyhow? Potatoes, right? Hey, summer's short enough without having to spend it in misery in the middle of nowhere in a tent with no toilet.

But, of course, Dad doesn't see it this way. Oh, no. He doesn't understand that family vacations suck for kids my age. He says, "Idaho is beautiful and peaceful and it'll be like a nice place for the family to get to know each other." Hey, like I don't already know my own family? And besides, while the family's getting to know each other, Larry will be getting to know Susan Jamison because I won't be around to keep an eye on him. Susan Jamison. Sneaky little bitch!

When I try to explain that I'm old enough to stay home alone and that all my friends are here and that backpacking isn't my thing and that Norman is a potential mass murderer, he goes and flies off in all directions. He says, "Listen, Shirley, this is our vacation, and you're going to enjoy it whether you like it or not." Can you believe this? How 'bout this for screwed-up logic? Parents become major-league airheads when they don't want to listen to reason.

So, I guess I gotta go to Idaho and play like another potato for a couple of weeks. While you guys are all here living like civilized, normal human beings, hanging out at the mall and partying, I'll be walking to the john in the wilderness someplace hand in hand with a grizzly bear. You've got it made, you know that, Sharon? You're lucky your parents are divorced.

DARLENE

She bemoans the loss of her pet.

I know you may think this is off the wall, but I'm really bummed out because my dog died last week. It's kind of like I'm running on empty, you know. It's like somebody has pulled a plug in my head and drained all the happiness out.

I had Curly since I was ten years old. He was a neat pet who never barked and went ape or caused us any trouble. He was a nice animal, and I really loved him a lot. If you can understand that. A person can get really attached to their pets, you know. Can get as attached to them as you do to a person.

People who've never had animals around have no concept of the closeness you can develop for them and how you look forward to seeing them every day and how you miss them when you're away. You develop like this strong bond between you, this special connection. Like between Curly and me. He'd be waiting for me every evening when I came home from school, and he'd hang around when I was doing homework and stuff. And he slept in my room every night. He'd curl up at the foot of my bed and stay there till morning. When I got cold, I used to slip my feet under him to keep them warm. Since he died, I haven't hardly slept at all. There's this big empty space now that Curly used to fill.

We got Curly from the pound when he was just a puppy. I picked him out of a litter because he had this large brown spot over one eye. He wasn't a thoroughbred, no way. Just a mutt. Who knows how many crossbreeds. "A Heinz 57," my dad used to say. But he was smart and perceptive and always alert and playful. Mutts are often exceptionally intelligent dogs. And he had this great temperament. And he was cool, too. He had this laid-back attitude. But he knew what was happening. You didn't put anything over on Curly. He was hip. Like I said, cool. Kind of a Spuds McKenzie type, you know.

One of the neat things about animals is that they aren't demanding. They're just there, always there for you. And they don't ask a lot. Just a little attention every now and then. A kind word. Some playfulness. And there is this special quality to their silence when they're nearby. It's a quietness that allows you to be relaxed in their company without a lot of phony bull. A quality people should develop in their relationships, I think.

Curly had been sick for a long time, and we'd had him to the vet's often. But he wasn't getting any better. The last time we took him in, the vet said that we should put him to sleep, that he was suffering, and that he wasn't going to recover. So we left him there. And I left part of myself there with him, too.

I sure do miss that dog.

CINDY

Cindy's mother is addicted to the Home Shopping Network, a habit Cindy finds extravagant and downright obscene.

Okay, like here she sits by the hour ordering up this garbage from the Home Shopping Network, okay? A boat-load of bull-shit crap that she'll toss out in six months. It's really a bizarre trip, let me tell you, Darlene. Bizarre! Have you ever caught it? Home Shopping? Hey, it's going on night and day. And they advertise all this junk like you won't believe. Like last night they're hyping these little ceramic dolls that look like the crappy little figurines they have on sale all the time at discount stores. And my mother flips for them. She goes and orders three of them. One looks like Porky Pig in drag. One looks exactly like Norma Anderson. And you know how ugly *she* is! And one looks like this painted-up, puppet-faced little dork-ball. But Mom thinks they're cute. She's got this whole case jammed full of these turkeys, and if you touch one she goes nuts. Like if you broke one you'd be trashing the Crown Jewels.

She sits in front of the TV all day checking out the trash they sell. Gimmick stuff: Like hair driers that have built-in radios and stuffed animals that are actually handbags. She bought this gross little hippo with a zipper in its back that she carries all the time. I won't leave the house with her when she carries it. Since she found Home Shopping, she's become crazed,

Darlene. Her mind is wasted, I swear. She's become like this Home Shopping robot, or something. Some days I think I'm part of this crazy Home Shopping sci-fi movie.

I don't dare bring her habit up in front of my father. If I do, later she accuses me of ratting on her. Dad told her if she doesn't cool it with buying all the crap, he's going to cancel all our credit cards. Last month the Master Charge was over two thousand dollars! Two thousand bucks for stuffed-hippo purses and musical plant hangers and genuine imitation-crystal rabbits and gold-plated miniature horseshoes that you use for coasters. It's insane. She's lost it. Totally lost it. Come on over sometime and watch her while she's watching the show. She's like on another planet. Gone. Zappo. Here she sits holding the telephone with these weird eyes like some whacked-out zombie. I'm talking "Twilight Zone" here, Darlene. (*She imitates the* "Twilight Zone" *theme music.*)

And guess what? This week she's Home Shopping for Christmas. Christmas! And here it is only June. She says she wants to get the good stuff before it's all gone. "Good stuff." She kidding? As if there is any. God only knows what we'll be getting this year. I hate to think about it. I have like this gnawing feeling it's going to be a strange Christmas, that I'm going to open up my gift and there it'll be—one of those damned hippo purses.

MARCIE

Financial realities are impediments to Marcie's going to camp. But she is understanding and supportive.

It's like this: My father has been out of work for almost six months now. They laid him off because things were slow at the factory. They laid off over three thousand people down there. The whole town is suffering because of it.

Up 'til now, we've always had everything we've ever needed. Probably more, I think. We've always lived really well. And my mother has never had to work because my father has always had a good job. Before he was laid off, he supervised a whole group.

The day he was fired was a very unsettling day for all of us. Unsettling most of all, I think, because of the way it affected my father. The whole thing really brought him down. He's usually this cheerful, happy-go-lucky type of person who is the last one to complain or be upset by problems. When everybody else is in the dumps, he's always the one who cheers them up and gets things back on track, you know. He's an optimist. At least he used to be, anyway. Now, I'm not sure.

It seems that being fired changed him, altered him. He's just not what he used to be. Not like before. It's like there is this . . . this something missing in him, you know. Like some vital part. Like this something important was taken right out of him. I guess it's his feeling of dignity and self-respect. And then there has to be lots of pressure. You can see it in him.

He's been all over town looking for work. He's even sent résumés to companies out of town. But so far, nothing. Only offers for stupid jobs that won't pay enough to support the family. Some nights when he comes home from interviews and job hunting, he just sits in his chair and doesn't speak to anyone. He just sits and looks off into space. Even though he doesn't say anything, you can tell he's hurting. It's really sad.

Last week, Mom took a job at Smith & Webster's department store. She'll be working in the accounting department. And my brother got this job down at Henderson's hardware. We're all pitching in. It's the least we can do. At a time like this, a family has to pull together.

So this year I won't be going to camp. Hey, the way things are, camp is out of the question. Instead, I'll be working part-time at McDonald's. Who knows, maybe it'll be better than goofing off all summer, anyhow. Already just the thought of being able to help out is a lot more uplifting than the thought of sitting around roasting marshmallows for three weeks. Besides, the mosquitoes eat me alive.

ANNIE

Annie, now living in a foster home, is still afraid that she will be abducted by her father.

Both of my parents were druggies. They were strung out most of the time. And when they were, they neglected me. Totally. When they were high, they didn't give a damn. A lot of the time there was no food in the house. The place was a pit hole. Stinking. Dirty. We lived like pigs. That's the way it is with addicts, they only care about one thing—getting their hands on drugs. And they'll do anything to get it. Anything. My mother even sold my clothes to get drug money. They were sick people, my parents. Sick as hell.

I would come home from school some days and find my mother and father so stoned they'd be passed out in the middle of their bed. Then, one day, I come home and find my mom dead on the kitchen floor. My dad was just sitting there, stoned, out of it. I don't think he was even aware that she'd died. I went into shock. When I began to cry, he started slapping me around and going crazy and screaming. He was hysterical and out of control. I ran out the back door and went to my aunt's and uncle's and stayed there as long as I could. They knew what was going on and tried to protect me and keep me from Dad as long as they could. But eventually I had to go back home.

After Mom was gone, Dad got even heavier into drugs. And he began to abuse me. He'd beat me for no reason, as if it were my fault he was a junkie. He treated me like hell. So I told my aunt and uncle, and they they told Dad they were going to call the authorities. He came unglued and panicked and kidnapped me because he was afraid they were going to take me away. We drove around the country for almost three weeks, living in cheap motels. It was like this nightmare with him slapping me around and cursing, and doing drugs all day long. And by now I hated him. I hated my own father.

When we finally came home he told me that if I ever tried to make trouble again he'd kill me. I was scared to death. God only knows what he'd do when he was bombed. He wouldn't let anyone see me and wouldn't let me answer the phone. I lived in constant fear and couldn't sleep. After a few weeks of living like this prisoner I just had to break away, had to get out. So I ran off to my aunt's and uncle's again and talked them into contacting the authorities and telling them what was happening. The authorities put me in my aunt's and uncle's custody and issued a restraining order against my dad.

I'm beginning to readjust, finally. I'm doing okay in school and I'm into a bunch of activities. But I still don't trust adults. Not completely. And why should I? I mean . . . look how they've treated me.

BETTY

Unfortunately, Betty, an average, healthy teenager, is under pressure from overachieving parents.

Look, I mean I don't mean to say I have the intellect of a chicken. What I'm saying here is that I'm not Einstein, you know. I'm like this normal person who is just me, that's all. What am I supposed to be here, anyway, this super brain who is supposed to figure out the theory of relativity while juggling chain saws? I mean . . . c'mon, gimme a break.

It's not enough that I carry a "B" average. Nooo . . . I have to get "A's" because my mother and father got "A's." All I ever hear is about how they were at the top of their classes in high school and college; how they were National Honor Roll students; how they got scholarships; how they used to sit around and read poetry to each other and listen to Mozart. Can you imagine what would happen if I suggested to Ralph we sit around and rattle off poetry and listen to classical music? He'd be outta here. And who could blame him?

My dad's all pissed because I'm not on the debating team. He just can't get it through his head that I hate public speaking. Every time I have to get up in front of people. I break out in a cold sweat and my hands get clammy and my heart pounds so hard you can hear it in the next block. Dad says debating will help me think on my feet. No way. Debating helps me *faint* on my feet.

My parents are both overachievers. My mom, for example, is head of the local chamber of commerce and the Democratic Party. Plus she's on the board at the hospital and is an active fund raiser for the local library. Plus, she takes care of the house, knits, plays a great game of tennis, and can whip up a killer soufflé. There isn't anything she can't do, anything. She could write the phone book on the head of a pin blindfolded if she set her mind to it. And my dad is the president of his company, a scratch golfer, a volunteer fireman, chairman for the United Fund, and is on the planning committee for the city. He reads the *New York Times* from cover to cover every day, knocks off a book before bedtime, and figures out his income tax in his head. Somtimes I think my parents aren't human.

And here I am, this lowly "B" student whose idea of an intellectual evening is a pizza with everything, a couple of Classic Cokes, and a few new CDs. I haven't got a chance. I'm doomed. I'll never be able to measure up.

You know, sometimes I think I'm not their daughter, that there must have been a mix-up at the hospital. Somewhere in the country today there is this super-brainy genius of a kid living with parents who are a couple of normal nerds.

MARY

Mary, a teen alcoholic, tells of her problem.

I'm an alcoholic. With some kids it's drugs. With me it's alcohol. Yeah, you heard right, I'm an alcoholic, a card-carrying member of AA.

Both of my parents are alcoholics. From as far back as I can remember, drinking was a big part of the family scene. Booze was everywhere. They say when you grow up in this kind of environment, you're more inclined to be a drinker yourself. And then there's the genetic angle. Often it's part of the genetic makeup, a kind of alcoholic heritage. Although I can't stand around blaming genetics and my parents. Because blame doesn't solve anything. Blaming is just a cop-out to avoid looking into yourself, you know. Blame sucks.

But you can only avoid coming to grips with the problem for so long. If you don't, you'll wind up trashing your life. I almost hit the bottom myself. Even at my age, I was in big-time trouble because alcohol had a hold on me and I was letting it ruin my life. It was as though it had this spell on me, this . . . this hold. I was totally into it. It was this strong, overpowering, destructive thing pulling me down further and further every day.

We always had booze around the house. My parents had this well-stocked bar in their rec room where they had these bashes where everybody got smashed. This is where I started drinking. They used to let me have beer because they thought it was cute to see a kid drink. And I liked the way it tasted. Right from the first, I liked the taste of alcohol. And, like I said, they thought it was fun to see me drink. A real joke, huh? Only trouble is, the joke was on me.

Then I started drinking when they weren't around. I'd sneak off to the bar and have a beer or two. Then I started experimenting with the hard stuff. After a while, I couldn't be without it. I craved it. Sometimes I'd wake up in the middle of the night thinking about it and sneak down and pour myself a drink.

Alcohol seemed to make things better. Things I was afraid of seemed to be easier when I was drinking. I'd drink before dates and before exams, anytime I felt nervous or unsure. I felt safe whenever I crawled into the bottle. To the point where I was loaded a lot of the time and getting into more and more scrapes— like wrecking cars and waking up in strange places. I was on a slide. I was in serious trouble. I was on my way down. But I pulled out. Thank God I pulled out. I got into AA with my parents. Now we're all sober. Have been for some time.

It sure is neat waking up knowing that you're sober and free.

JILL

Jill thinks Tony is hot but Tony is interested in her best friend, Laura. Here, she relates her dilemma.

So Laura comes over to me at the dance and says, "Isn't Tony cute?" and I say, "Yeah." Because Tony is the coolest guy around. Then she says, "Do you think I should ask him to dance." And I say, "Sure, why not?" But she says she's too bashful, that I should ask him to dance. And I say, "Hey, why me? You're the one who wants to dance with him." And she says, "Yeah, but you've got all kinds of nerve,, and stuff like this doesn't bother you." And I say, 'But what'll it prove if I dance with him?" And she says, "While you're dancing with him, you can tell him that I think he's cute and ask him to dance the next dance with me." Now I'm thinking that this whole thing is pretty far out, but because I'm Laura's best friend, I ask Tony to dance. Wow, was he ever a good dancer.

Okay. So while we're dancing, I ask him if he'll dance with Laura because Laura thinks he's cute and he says, "Sure." So, after the dance, I go and tell Laura that he'll dance with her, and she is real thrilled like some stupid grade-school dope and gets so red in the face that she looks like a stop-light. So then Tony comes on over and asks Laura to dance, and she says, "No thanks, I don't dance with strangers." And Tony walks away. "No thanks?" I can't believe this. After all this, she turns the guy down like he's a plate of Hamburger Helper. I say, "Hey, Laura, what's going on here? Are you crazy? After asking me to dance and go through all this you tell the guy to get lost?" And Laura says, "This way he'll think I'm hard to get and will be more attracted to me."

And do you know what? She was right. After that, he couldn't stay away from her. He kept bugging her to dance with him all night long. And she kept turning him down. Then, next day, he starts calling her all the time and asking her out. After about two weeks she agrees to go out with him, and they've been going steady ever since.

Tony is really hot. Like I said, he's the coolest guy around. He has this way about him. And you should see the way he dresses. He is always styled out. I'm crazy about him. But so far as he's concerned, forget it. I don't exist. He looks right through me. I might as well be a pane of glass. And besides, what can I do, anyway? I can't make a move on him because Laura's my best friend. Even though she did use me to get to Tony. Sometimes, when I think about it, I get really upset. But then, on the other hand, I have to respect her for her knowledge of the male ego.

AMANDA

The death of her mother, the realization of it, her deepest feelings, underpin this speech.

At first there is this terrible shock, and you're sick and shattered. Then there is this period where you are more or less numb; with people coming by the house and telephoning and bringing in food. It's like you're in this kind of unreal state, half sleeping, half awake. Then there is the preparing for the funeral. You go with your father to pick out the casket. You listen to the undertaker talk to your dad very quietly. About her makeup, her clothing, the flowers. He's sympathetic but also very professional and cold. This is when the realities begin to set in and your mind races and just thinking makes you hurt inside.

Then there's the funeral home. For two afternoons and evenings you're there. People come and say nice things and you nod respectfully and they sign the register and leave. You watch them through the windows as they go off to their cars. You see them talking, laughing, making plans. Already their minds are off of my mother. They've come by, paid their respects, and they're back to living again.

At the cemetery, you see some of them again. Those who had been especially close, the real friends. The sun is hot on my back, and I can feel the perspiration running down my sides. It is so quiet I can hear my heart pounding. The only sound is the wind moving the trees. A few words are said over the casket. I don't remember them because I wasn't listening. I didn't give a damn about the words; I just wanted her back.

Afterwards, we go home and sit in the kitchen. My father, my brothers, and I. We don't say much. And there is so much to say. We just sit there in silence. I feel like bursting. I'm so full of feelings.

The house is like this shadow of what it was when she was alive. But, you know, Mother is still around because she's in my memories. I hear her laughing and calling our names and talking with Aunt Julie on the phone. I hear her footsteps on the porch; I hear her snapping out pillow slips upstairs while humming this little tune. She's gone but she's still here. She's everywhere.

As time passes, the sadness passes, too. Every day you come a little more out of the fog, you know. As the days pass, you get back your laughter and get on with living. But there is still like this emptiness. Maybe there always will be. But slowly you adjust to it. Like they say—life goes on. But she'll always be here, always. Her spirit will never die.

KATE

Several years ago, Kate was molested by her neighbor and then, not long after that, was sexually abused by her mother's boyfriend. Her mother, however, refused to believe that either incident ever took place.

It all started when I was just twelve years old, living with my mother and her boyfriend. I used to be home alone a lot because my mother had to work. Well, one day, this guy, Bob, our neighbor, comes over, okay? He was like this friend of my mom's, and he knew that the key to the house was hidden in the flower-pot near the front door. Anyway, he came in and came up to me while I was watching television. I didn't pay much attention to him because I knew him and was used to him being around. But this particular day, he was acting very strange. He came over and sat next to me on the couch and began running his hand up and down my leg. Then he became bolder, forcing his hand under my jeans and . . . and . . . well, he was touching me, you know. I tried my best to get away from him, but he kept forcing himself on me and pulling at my clothes. And then . . . then he exposed himself.

When I told my mother what had happened, she said I was making it up, that Bob was a nice guy and a good neighbor and would never think of doing anything like that. As hard as I tried to convince her she wouldn't believe my story.

The next time it was much worse and involved my mother's boyfriend, who was living with us part of the time. One night, while my mother was away, he came into my bedroom while I was doing homework and began forcing himself on me. I tried to keep him away, but he was a big man and I didn't have a chance. When I resisted, he began to slap me. I was scared to death. He had this terrible temper. I didn't know what the hell he might do. He tore off my robe and then . . . then . . . well, I was sexually abused.

When my mother came home, I told her what had happened, and she refused to believe it. She said I must have this problem where I have to make up these far-out, fantastic stories. First about Bob and now about her boyfriend. She called me a lying little slut and a little troublemaker. I knew right then that I couldn't live in my own home anymore. It was too dangerous. I had to get out.

I'm living with my father now. I was in a bunch of foster homes, but I ran away each time to be with my dad. Even though he has a drinking problem, they've finally decided that it's better for me to be with him than to be with strangers. Besides, he treats me good and I feel safe with him. He's a nice man. He may be an alcoholic, but I know he loves me.

BARBARA

Barbara is put off by her mother's outrageous dietetic demands.

My mother has this totally insane attitude about food. She eats like a bird—a hummingbird. For breakfast, she'll have a piece of dry toast and coffee. For lunch, a salad with no dressing. For dinner, a thimble-full of chicken. It's like her whole life is a diet, you know. When we go to a restaurant, she pulls out this little booklet that tells you how many calories there are in food, how much fat, how many carbs and stuff. Sitting down to eat with my mother is like sitting down at the table with a scientist. She analyzes everything. And of course this means I have to eat rabbit food, too. The last time we had lunch, she insisted I order a cucumber salad and a tomato stuffed with tuna. Oh yeah, and iced tea. Cucumbers and iced tea. Real appetizing, huh? Puke-ola! This is why I try to avoid eating with her at all costs.

She's constantly bugging me about what I eat. "Don't eat fat. Don't eat meat. Don't eat sweets. Don't eat processed food." *Don't* is a big word in my mom's dietary vocabulary. And I'm not fat. Hey, I'm not even overweight. I mean, if I was like this balloon or something, it'd be different.

She's always jumping on my dad for what he eats, too. The poor guy can't enjoy a meal without hearing how unhealthy everything he's eating is. She gets into all kinds of facts and figures: about how many of the calories you're eating are fat;

about how pesticides cause cancer; about how meat-packing plants aren't sanitary; about these laboratory experiments on rats. She's like this walking, talking, food horror picture. Her conversation alone could cause a person to lose weight. I mean, how can you possibly eat when someone's sitting talking about rats shriveling up and dying because they don't get enough protein? Hey, the thought of rats healthy is gross enough.

Mom used to be overweight. I guess this is the reason she's flipped on diet. Because she's a former fatty. She's a reformed food junkie. Which is okay to a point, all right? But she's really taken the whole thing out of sight. To the point where she's paranoid about food. I'll bet if you hid a Twinkie in her purse she'd have a stroke.

I think eating right is sensible and being healthy is important. But like who needs taking it to extremes? It's important to enjoy life, too. I mean, hey, we're not supposed to put our life in a Ziploc bag, you know. I think common sense is the answer. With food and everything else, it's just a matter of balance. Besides, how about the thought of going through life without another cheeseburger?

ELLEN

Ellen feels it time to talk openly with her parents about AIDS.

Please! This isn't the Dark Ages. This isn't the time of the Inquisition or the Salem Witch Trials. Or maybe it is! Yeah, maybe it damned well is. The way you two go around speaking under your breath in hushed tones about the subject is ridiculous. You think I don't know about AIDS? You think I don't read, don't watch TV? You think I'm some blind and dumb teenager whose head is into nothing but rock 'n' roll? You know what? You remind me of my teachers. They skirt the subject, too. Oh yeah, we have these "informative" discussions. The only problem is—they're not informative. They circle the guts of the issue. It's like this cosmetic treatment, you know. This very careful, eggshell clinical discussion where everyone's afraid to talk plain. You think this is learning? You think this is healthy? You think this is enlightening? Hell, no! It's avoidance!

Like Jerry Raynor, our neighbor. You actually think I believe he died of pneumonia? C'mon, the man was a homosexual. He had AIDS! The man died because his body was ravaged by the damned disease. Because the poor guy was infected by an active HIV virus. Pneumonia! Pfft! Gimme a break. You and the rest of the neighborhood have your heads so far in the sand it's pitiful. And what did any of you do for the poor man? Nothing? And why? Well, I'll tell you why.

Because of your prejudice, that's why. Because of your fears! Because of your stupid, old- fashioned ideas! So the guy goes and dies without anyone reaching out to him because you were all so afraid that it would taint you all in some crazy way. Or maybe you were afraid you would "catch it!" I would laugh if it wasn't so pitiful.

Sometimes I wonder who the clear thinkers are in this society. Certainly not many of the so-called "adults," that's for damned sure. A person has to be emotionally mature before he can be considered an adult. He has to get hold of some enlightenment. He has to face up to reality.

I get it here, I get it in school, I seem to get it everywhere. It's like some conspiracy against me, my generation. It's no wonder so many young people rebel. When you live with dishonesty for so long you've got to do something!

YOUNG MEN

JERRY

Jerry's sister and her baby have recently succumbed to AIDS.
Here, Jerry speaks of the incident.

My sister, Janet, was just twenty-seven when she found out she had AIDS. She'd been feeling sick and tired for a long time and was developing these sores in her mouth. In fact, at first, the doctors didn't think of testing her for AIDS because she was married and had a baby. They just assumed it was a virus.

After she found out what was wrong, she told people around here that she was suffering from leukemia. Her husband, Cal, a carpenter, was the one who made up this lie because he was afraid if people knew the truth, they wouldn't use his services. Then, when their baby was a year old, they discovered it had AIDS, too. And they made up the same story, that the baby was suffering from leukemia also. This is how ashamed and guilty they felt. And I can understand. People around here have got some pretty straight-laced ideas, you know. So, Jan and Cal became locked into living this lie because they were afraid of what people might think.

But all of this secrecy and living this awful lie started to take its toll. Cal, who was an alcoholic, started to drink again, and Janet felt like she was being cheated out of life. Finally, about a year after she'd learned she had AIDS, Janet joined a group where she stood up and told everyone the truth. Afterwards, she said she finally felt relieved and relaxed and at ease. And her honesty seemed to relieve her fears, too. But for Cal, well,

her coming out really hit him hard. He drank heavier and became more and more private and withdrawn. Then, last April,
he went into his workshop and shot himself. In his suicide note,
he said, "I just couldn't it handle it anymore. I'm tired of running." That's how ashamed he was.

Janet died in September and her baby died just three weeks
later.

During the last four months of her life, Janet spoke out
about AIDS. She wanted people to know more about it and not
be afraid of it or of the people who carry it. She became a real
campaigner so that people would realize that AIDS is a disease,
not a stigma, something you should run from and cover up for.
She wanted people to stop judging. She told them that it didn't
matter how people got AIDS—she'd gotten hers from tainted
blood from a transfusion after an appendectomy. She told them
that what matters is that people who have AIDS have a disease
and that we should be understanding and give them love.

My sister was one hell of a person.

DAVID

David responds negatively to the suggestion that he should date the local brain.

Hey, how about you? Why don't you date Irma Peterson, okay? I mean, if you're so red hot for Irma Peterson, why aren't you taking her out? (*Beat.*) Oh yeah, sure, sure, tell me another one. "Because she's a bad dancer." Yeah, right. Anyway, how would you know? Like how many times have you danced with her, anyhow? Besides, you can't dance. You dance like a spastic robot. Face it, the reason you don't want to make it with Irma Peterson is because she's like this walking encyclopedia, that's why. That's why nobody wants to take her out. Because it's like taking out a library. Once you date Irma Peterson is the last time you date Irma Peterson. Hey, I know from personal experience. Irma Peterson is the date from hell.

I took her out about three months ago. To a movie. Cost seven bucks apiece plus parking and popcorn and Cokes. And do I get to hear the movie? No way. I get to hear Irma Peterson, movie reviewer. I can't tell you what the picture was about because Irma Peterson was leaning into my ear all night about a bunch of stupid intellectual garbage. Who the hell is Kurosawa, anyway? She kept talking about this dude and comparing the movie to one he made. Something called *Rashomon.* It takes place in medieval Japan. It's supposed to be this masterpiece. If it's so great, how come I've never heard of it?

Then, after fifteen bucks plus parking, popcorn, and Cokes, she has the nerve to accuse me of not being intellectually inquisitive. Hey, like everyone's supposed to know all about medieval Japan, right? All most people know about Japan is that this is where Toyotas come from. Toyotas and Hondas. What else is to know? And, oh yeah, Walkman.

She says the picture's convoluted and that the main guy's motivation is weak. Whatever this means. Who knows what she's talking about? And with her yelling in my ear, who would know if there was a plot or not? Then the crazy bitch goes off on this tangent about something that Alfred Hitchcock did called *The 39 Steps*. How it's like, and I'm using her exact words—"This unparalleled use of timing and comic relief juxtaposed against a 1930s English milieu." If you wanna know how I remember this, it's because she repeated it in my ear at very close range about thirty times. To the point where the people in front of us were turning around and flipping us off.

I wouldn't date Irma Peterson again for anything. Because she's a smart-ass-know-it-all-motor-mouth. And the sad thing of it is, she's beautiful. Which goes to prove, beauty's only skin deep.

DAN

Even though the divorce of his parents presents problems, Dan believes the dissolution is necessary.

It's nothing new. My parents have been talking about getting a divorce for years. They bring it up every time they have an argument. Which is often. For no apparent reason, they get into these wild, screaming, off-the-wall arguments all the time, accusing each other of the damnedest things, laying blame, cursing. They spin out, go completely out of control. Worse than kids anytime.

And you can hear them all over hell, all over the neighborhood. In a way, this is the worst part, you know. The fact that the neighbors can hear them. It's really embarrassing that the whole neighborhood can hear your parents fighting. Then, for a while afterwards, after they have these terrible brawls, they go through these periods where they treat each other okay. It's like this is their way of making up for the screaming and all the crummy things they said to each other. It's like they call a truce. But the truce never lasts very long. Before you know it, they're fighting again. And the periods between their fights have gotten shorter. To the point now where it seems like they're at each other's throats constantly.

I think the hardest thing for me to understand is how they can be so hateful to each other. The things they say you wouldn't say to a dog. It's almost as if they hate each other's guts, or something. Maybe they do.

I think about my parents a lot, you know. About how sad it is they've lost all respect for each other. It couldn't have always been like this. I'm sure that at one time or other, when they were young, they were in love. After all, isn't this is the reason people get married? Because they love each other and want to make a life together? Because they're in love and willing to make a lasting commitment?

But what happens along the way to make them get to this point? What goes wrong? I think maybe it's little things. Little lies. Little indiscretions. Small slights. Offhand remarks that would be better off not said. I guess it's this and a lot more things that add up to emotions going out of control.

I used to hate the thought of my parents splitting up. Just the threat of it, the insecurity of the whole thing turned me around and really messed with my head. But lately, lately I think that it'd be the best thing for everyone. For them, for me, and my sister, Carrie—everybody. It's no good for people to live around constant hostility. When there's no more love, only meanness and hatred, what the hell's the point of going on?

JAMES

Physical exercise isn't for James.

I mean like, hey, I like to look good, too, you know. I mean, I don't wanna look like some bag of meatballs either, okay? But I also don't wanna look like some no-neck gorilla, some over-built goon. Being super huge is stupid.

We've got these guys in school who work out in the gym every day, you know. Most of 'em are jocks, muscle-heads. I see them down there sweating like pigs, pumping all this iron like crazy, doing clean-and-jerks and bench presses and curls and stuff. Here they are, grunting and groaning like animals. And you should see they way they look. Like these big sacks of cement on two legs. One guy, Jerry Mendez, is so musclebound he can't even walk right. He waddles around like a drunken duck, or something. And he's got this neck as wide as his head. The guy's more ape than person.

As for me, I like being built regular, you know. Normal. And besides, I'm not into cracking myself up and having sore tendons and bad knees when I'm twenty. The muscle-heads have this expression, "No pain, no gain," okay? Well, the way I see it is, "Feel pain, no brain." Pain is like this built-in thing that keeps us from messing ourselves up. It's like nature's way of saying, "Easy pal." Pain is like nature's governor, you know. I try to keep my weight down and stay on the thin side. A guy who's thin looks much better in his clothes. You take a look back at your old-time cool movie stars, and they were all on the thin side. Guys like Fred Astaire and Cary Grant and Gary Cooper and like that. And I never heard of any of those guys pumping iron and busting their buns in gyms. They were out somewhere in tailor-made tuxedos getting it on with the dames.

I tried pumping iron just once. Jerry Franks hyped me on working out with him. Jerry is built like this rhino, you know. He grabs this ton of steel off this rack and pushes it over his head. The veins in his face stood out so far it looked like they were going to pop. And his face turned this dark shade of purple—like rotten eggplant. He goes and pumps this truck- load of steel about ten times, okay? Then he hands me this loaded barbell, and it's so heavy I almost go through the floor. He tells me to curl it in my arms. Says it'll make my biceps bigger. I did about two curls, and the pain was so great even my Nikes hurt. I told him to forget it. I wasn't about to go blowing out my bones for nothing.

Another thing—girls don't like musclebound guys. They've told me so. Over-developed guys turn them off. What they like is normal-sized guys with nice butts. If you've got a nice butt, you can go a long way with the babes. Something that's more important than having big arms any day.

HAROLD

Harold, an accident victim, now paralyzed, tells of his ordeal.

(*Limping forward.*) Hey, it's . . . it's not easy to talk about, you know. I mean. . . . (*He finds the words difficult.*) Up 'til now, I haven't told anyone; anyone outside my family, that is.

I was out cruising with Fred and Cliff. We always cruised on Saturday nights. It was like our thing. Like lots of people hit the streets on the weekend, you know. This is where it's happening. This is where you see your friends and talk to the girls. Everybody does it.

The big mistake was the drinking. We'd had a few beers at my place and then stopped off at a carry-out and picked up a twelve- pack. We were pretty blitzed, I guess. But, what the hell, I mean...we were having fun, I mean. . . . You don't think you're as loaded as you really are.

We were in Fred's Camaro. It was a hot car and Fred could really burn it. We got into this thing with some guys and these babes in this 5.0 Mustang and they challenged us, okay? Said they could wipe us. So Fred punched it, and we took off for the canyon out off of Route 56. The canyon is a cool place to race. It has lots of curves and like this long tunnel you can blast through blowing your horn.

It was around midnight when we hit the canyon. We must have been going ninety with the Mustang right behind. The Mustang was really hot and the guy kept trying to pass us, but

Jerry kept swerving back an' forth so he couldn't get by. But the guy was an ace driver, and when there was this opening, he blew us off. This really got Fred pissed. He jammed it and we were right on top of the Mustang at about a hundred miles per hour. The Camaro was singing, man, singing. Wow! Then, on this long, sweeping curve right before the tunnel, Fred makes his move by cutting inside the Mustang, okay? But just as we're passing, Fred loses it and we break away and shoot over the side of the road. All I remember is like the world being upside down for a few seconds. The cops say we plunged over two hundred feet.

Both Fred and Cliff were pronounced dead at the scene. I was airlifted to the hospital with critical injuries, where I was in surgery for over five hours. For a while, it was touch-and-go. They didn't think I was going to make it. I was busted up pretty good. I was in a body cast for four months, and I'm partially paralyzed on my left side. Maybe with therapy I'll gain back some feeling. They're not sure.

I'm pretty lucky, I guess. Even though I'm half a person . . . I'm still alive.

BEN

Ben, the son of a working single parent, experiences loneliness.

My mother and father were divorced two years ago, and because of my father's drinking problem I live with my mom. She's a salesperson for this big clothing manufacturer in New York, and her job requires her to travel a lot. She covers three states—Ohio, Michigan, and Illinois.

At first I thought it was neat that she was gone a lot. I mean, I get to be here alone, I can do what I want, I can stay up late, hang out, have friends in, whatever. I have total freedom. For a young guy, it has to be like this perfect situation, right? Like this dream life. And all of my friends envy me. They tell me all the time how I've got it made, how lucky I am, you know. They say that they'd love for their parents to take off and leave them home alone. Then they could party all they wanted and not have to do a lot of stupid regimented crap. They all wish they had the freedom I do.

But more and more, as time goes on, I'm starting to think maybe they're the ones who have it made, not me. When I go to their homes, it feels different. They feel like . . . like . . . they feel like *homes*. Here, to be honest, it doesn't feel like anything. It's just this empty, vacant, nothing. It's just a . . . just a big nothing place. I mean, yeah, it's a nice house, furnished nice and all that, sure. But it doesn't have any warmth, any feelings. At least, when my parents were together, even though they got into major hassles, at least then it felt like a home.

You know, after a while, all the partying and hanging out, the freedom isn't so cool anymore. I mean, how long you can goof off and party? Not that I'm against freedom. No way, not at all. Freedom's important. Freedom is part of us, one of the greatest things in life. But when there's freedom without sharing, without caring, what the hell's the good of it, anyway?

I guess what I'm saying here is that a lot of the time I'm lonely. So lonely that I actually ache inside. Yeah, I really do, sometimes I actually hurt from loneliness. Sometimes when I come home to this empty place, or after a party, after everyone has gone, I get super down, super depressed. And a guy my age shouldn't feel lonely, and empty, and depressed, you know. Hey, it's not right.

I know that my lifestyle looks good to my friends, but they don't realize; they don't realize that they're the ones who have it made. I may have this so-called freedom, but they have a family. They have people around who care.

RICK

Rick is fed up with his super-jock coach.

The coach is a nut, okay? He's a crazy, off-the-wall jock. He should have like this big "S" on the front of his sweatshirt for Super Jock. (*In a dramatic, radio voice.*) "Super Jock. He leaps tall students with a single bound. He's fast as a speeding basketball in the face. It's a bird, it's a plane, it's Super Jock!"

The guy's a nut altogether. Crazy! Making guys do a hundred push-ups. Making guys climb ropes to the top of the gym. Making guys run laps till their tongues are on their feet. Making guys do a thousand sit-ups. Making guys stand at attention in the hot sun. Making guys stick out their chests and pull in their guts. We're talking one sick, crazed dude.

The guy's this ex-Marine, okay? An old leatherneck. With a leather brain. He's got this "over the top," "do or die," "a few good men" mentality. He's like part Rambo and part John Wayne with a little Adolph Hitler thrown in just for the hell of it. He doesn't see us as young guys in a gym class; he sees us as recruits. Like this bunch of enlistees, okay? Get this: Last week he says, "I'm gonna turn you guys into men or hamburger casserole." He actually said that. And why? Because we couldn't run in place for fifteen minutes. Fifteen minutes! What the hell are we here, anyway, machines, or something?

His name is Benson. We all call him Major Benson because he's like this crazed military-type guy. Hey, you should get a load of the way he dresses: camouflage shirts and pants and OD tank tops and combat boots. He has his hair cut so short he looks like this big macho melon. And he drives around in this beat-up old Jeep with Marine insignias on it. What we're talking about here is a blood-and-guts and bullets freak. He's all the time talking about his gun collection. One of the guys saw it and says like his house is like this arsenal or armory, or something. He's got all kinds of ammo and automatic weapons. If World War III ever breaks out this dude can declare himself a separate country.

Taking gym is bad enough without having to have some wacko character out of *Apocalypse Now* standing over you and screaming, "Mister." Yeah, that's what he calls everyone, "Mister." Or, I should say, yells at everyone. He doesn't talk, man, not this guy, no way—he shouts. "Get down on that ground and give me a fast twenty, mister!" "Give me a fast ten laps, mister." I know what I'd like to give him. I'd like to give him a fast one right between his beady General Patton eyes.

Where the hell does the school board find these turkeys, anyway?

ERNIE

The sudden death of a parent has left deep emotional scars.

It happened four years ago. But it seems like it was only yesterday. Something like this never leaves you; it's always in the back of your mind. You go over and over it, relive it, and remember all the details. Like when they called me up to the office from class. I remember it vividly. When they told me my father had been killed in an auto accident, at first I couldn't grasp it. The initial impact of the thing was so shocking that I just couldn't get it into my head. My father was dead! My father was dead! Hey, parents don't die, other people die: neighbors, relatives, people you read about in the papers. But parents—they live forever! This is what you think because the thought of never seeing your mother or father again is out of the question.

For me, the news was too much to handle. I think now that you can be overwhelmed by too much reality. That something can happen that is *so* real, *so* big, *so* personal that you can't cope with it. I know that this is the way the news of my dad's death affected me. Jesus! My dad! I'd just seen him that morning. We'd talked like always and joked as usual and he drove off to work like always and. . . . Hell, he just couldn't be dead. But he was. But I chose not to believe it. Like I said, the reality was just too damned big.

After my father died, I became a different person—listless and depressed. I'd always been a good student, but after the tragedy, my grades went straight to hell. And I'd always been heavy into sports and had plenty of friends. But now, friends and sports didn't seem important to me anymore. I became more and more withdrawn and standoffish. Little by little, I became a loner. To where I started skipping school and avoiding people. Hey, it got to the point where I wouldn't even answer the phone.

My dad and I were very close. We did all kinds of things together. We were pals. He was a neat guy, someone I looked up to. I trusted him, respected him a lot. Then, alluva sudden, here he was gone. Alluva sudden I had no one I could trust. My mother tried to get me to relate to other men, wanted me to spend more time with my uncle. But it didn't work out. It just wasn't the same, you know. The only one I felt comfortable with was my mom. I wanted to be with her constantly. I didn't want to let her out of my sight because I was afraid if I did, something would happen to her, too. The thought of her dying like my dad drove me crazy.

It took a helluva long time for me to get over my fears and my feeling of emptiness. But, after a while, with my mother's and uncle's help and with the help of a few friends who would listen, I started getting myself together. Now, finally, I'm starting to live again.

DEAN

Dean likes to "play the field."

You've got like these guys who get hooked on just one babe, you know. They get all hot for like this one girl and they go get involved and before you know it they're going steady. Hey, you see them all the time. And it screws 'em up bad. Like take a look at Jim Ritter. Here you have your perfect example of a young guy who's already hen-pecked. He can't go anywhere without Dana Harris hanging on him. It's like they're hand-cuffed together or joined at the hip, or something. Just seeing them makes me realize how lucky I am.

The way I see it is, there are too many women around to get involved with just one babe. There are too many drawbacks. Like for example: Say you're going steady with this babe and you see another one who's neater, okay? What can you do, huh? Nothing, that's what. Nothing, because you're locked in, screwed, dead meat in the romance department. I mean, here you are like stuck with this dame and you can't put on any moves. 'Cause if you do, the babe you're going steady with gets all weird and comes off-the-wall and yells at you and makes you feel guilty. And hey, face it, man, guilt sucks.

I'm not putting any story on you here; I'm speaking from experience, okay? I've been through the steady routine a couple of times and I know where I'm coming from, okay? Remember when I dated Angela Campo? Whoa! (*He shivers at the thought.*) My life wasn't my own. I had no freedom. It was always like, "What are we doing tonight, Dean?" "How about coming over later, Dean?" "What you wanna do that for, Dean?" "You wanna go with Bob tonight? You just saw Bob last night, Dean." It was Dean this and Dean that to the point where I hated my own name. Not to mention seriously hating Angela Campo. And then, breaking up was sickening. When I gave her the dump, she went bananas and started accusing me of all kinds of crap—having other girlfriends and stuff. (*He shivers again.*) Like I said, guilt sucks.

How people stay married, I'll never know. I mean, even being around the same girl for a few nights is too much. A guy has to be nuts to tie himself down with just one bitch when he can take his pick from a bunch. And another thing, this way you never get bored and you don't feel obligated and feel you have to go to her house on Sunday and eat chicken and sit around with a bunch of overfed dorks.

Look, what's the hurry to get super tied-down at our age? Right now, while we're young, we should be enjoying our freedom, okay? There's plenty of time later to get married and settle down and live like a couch potato. When you're older, you're ready for it. Like my mom and dad. They seem to love boredom.

MARTIN

Because Martin is largely responsible for his younger sister and brother, he doesn't have much time for typical teen activities.

My dad left home a long time ago. He just walked out on us one day and never came back. We never hear from him. He never sends us a penny. It's like we don't exist.

In the beginning, it wasn't so bad because my mother was working. It was rough, but working together we got by okay. But then she became sick. Not physically sick, emotionally upset, psychologically unbalanced. The doctors think it has a lot to do with being faced with so much responsibility, with working and trying to raise three children. It was too much for her. She just couldn't hold up under the pressure, the constant financial problems. This is what they think is the biggest factor in her illness.

Now she's under psychiatric care for depression and spends most of the time in bed. Some days she's up, some down. You never know. Our social worker says she may be like this for a long time, that we shouldn't get our hopes too high. There are no guarantees, she tells us.

We get financial aid from the county. It isn't much, just enough to cover expenses. We never have much left over for extras.

My sister, Allison, is nine and my brother, Ronnie, is just two. This is the reason I don't have much time for regular teenage stuff, you know. Because I'm usually too busy filling the role of a parent. I guess you might say I'm kind of Allison's and Ronnie's teenage father. I have to dress my brother, give him his bath, get him ready for bed—do all the things you do for a two-year-old. I have to look after Allison, too. Even though she's nine, she still needs a lot of attention. I help her with her homework, spend time with her, take her places, watch out for her. When one of them is sick, I skip school to stay home and do the cooking, the marketing, and stuff.

I don't have much time for myself, can't do all the stuff most guys my age get to do. It's just not possible. No way. Not with all the work I have do at home. And there's a lot, too. But, even though it gets pretty crazy sometimes, I don't sit around on my butt bitching and complaining about my responsibilities. When there's something to be done, I just take it on and do it. Because I love my family. My family is my main priority.

Even though taking care of the house and my kid sister and brother is a pain sometimes, I think the rewards are pretty great. I mean, when you care about somebody, doing stuff for them is easy. (*Pause.*) I think the thing that bothers me most is how my dad could walk out on such neat people.

SAM

Roger's parents are leaving for the weekend. Here, Sam encourages him to the throw the "mother" of all parties.

Your folks are leaving for the whole weekend? You're kidding? Like for the whole weekend? (*Pause.*) Wow! All right! What a break, man. (*Pause.*) Why is it a break? Why is it a break? Are you for real here? Do you mean I have to tell you? Man, you've just been given two beautiful nights and three fantastic days of *total freedom*! It's like you're not going to be a prisoner for a change. (*Pause.*) Yeah, right—prisoner. What else do you think we are? Hey, Rog, face it, we're like a couple of convicts most of the time.

Look at it like this: Think of your home life as like this jail and of your dad as like the warden, okay? (*Pause.*) You never looked at it that way? It figures. Rog, sometimes you worry me. It's a damned good thing you've got me around to wise you up to what's happening, you know that?

So, anyway, like I was saying, most of the time it's like we're locked up in the can. We can't do this, we can't do that, we have to get clearance, permission to do everything. And when we wanna do something on our own, it's like being put on probation, okay? It's always like this big deal. Most of the time we're like under the watchful eyes of the prison guards, you know what I'm saying?

And now, now here, outta the blue, comes this golden opportunity. The warden and his wife have left for the weekend, and you have the keys to the joint in your back pocket. What a break. It's like you just got paroled or something, pal. (*Pause.*) You never looked at it that way? Will you stop saying that!?

Okay, so now you've got three days of freedom, okay? So what you gonna do with 'em? (*Pause.*) Hang around and watch TV? Are you crazy? Am I talking to a dope here, or something? What you do is like throw the biggest party this stupid town has ever seen. (*Pause.*) You don't know? Well, I do, and I'm saying we have the biggest blast in history. You can't let an opportunity like this go slipping through our—*your* hands. We invite everybody; we get in Jerry and his group; we invite babes, lotsa babes; we stock up on beverages; we load up on munchies; we rent videos; we get Dave to bring his twin cousins—the ones who look like Madonna; we get all kinds of decorations and party stuff and fix up this dump so it doesn't look like an overstuffed dungeon. Whaddaya think? (*Pause.*) You like it. Of course you like it! Who wouldn't like it?

So, okay, let's get our butts moving here. We've only got three days. Come Monday, it's back to San Quentin.

JIM

Jim's brother was the victim of an unprovoked attack.

The neighborhood is bad. It's been bad ever since I can remember. We've been planning to move for a long time, but my dad lost his job and, well . . . it just hasn't been possible.

Even though we live in a rough area where drug deals go down on every corner, we've always stayed clear of the problem, free of those people and their habits. We know what happens when you get into crack, marijuana, ice—any of the substances.

Bobby, my sisters, and I kept clear of the streets. We've always tried to be better than that. Because of our parents. Because of their concern for us and teaching us about the importance of staying out of trouble and of getting a proper education.

I'm a straight-A student. So was my brother, Bobby. He was at the top of his class, an honor student. He was one of the smartest guys you'd ever want to meet. He was a real neat person. Everybody liked him a lot. That's what's so shocking about it, about him being shot. It's such a waste, you know. I mean, if he'd been a person who was involved with drugs, involved with the gangs, you could understand why he might come to some trouble. But a guy like Bobby. . . . (*He shakes his head with disbelief.*)

It was all so crazy. We were just walking along, Bobby and I, minding our own business, when this car appears from out of nowhere. And then another car comes around a corner and cuts it off, slams into it. Then guys come piling out of the cars onto the street. They all have guns. They get into this huge argument, screaming and calling each other names. There was a lot of pushing and shoving—threats. Then this one kid challenges this guy from the other car, and the guy shoots him, just like that.

Then the other guys started blasting away. It was like a war out there, a war, I'm telling you, right there in the middle of the block with homes, families. . . . (*Pause.*) That's when Bobby got it. "I'm hit," he said, "they hit me." I turned to see him fall, holding his stomach.

At first they didn't think he would live. He was all torn up inside. But he made it, he beat the odds. But he's paralyzed from the waist down. Here he was, this great guy with this bright future with everything going for him, and now . . . now here he is with his life ripped apart. And for what? For nothing. It was senseless. What's happening to this world anyhow? Every time I think about it I get sick inside. Sick!

And I get goddamn mad!

LES

Les is not crazy about his part-time job.

My folks hassled me about getting a part-time job. Said I had to find out what work is all about. As if I don't know what work is all about. The way I figure it, work is this thing you hate that you do between being born and dying because this is what everybody has always done. But most people hate working, I think. Like my dad. He comes dragging ass home every night complaining about pressure and how he can't get people to work anymore and how his customers don't pay him and . . . hey, you name it. And when he's home, he can't relax because he's all the time thinking about his business. It's like the poor guy's this big workaholic-rat caught in this stupid trap, understand?

I know working keeps the economic system going. It's part of the old socioeconomic ballgame. So, everybody works, okay? But why? When I ask my dad this, he gets crazy and starts twisting the hair at his temples. He says, "What kind of a world would it be if nobody worked?" I tell him I think it'll be a better world because if nobody did anything, it would all even out. Besides, who knows what would happen because nobody's ever tried it? People have been work nuts since the dawn of time. Guys freezing their butts off in caves were busy screwing around with flint, for example. I think maybe like the work drive is a basic flaw in human nature.

But anyway, to keep my parents from bitching and ragging on me all the time, I go and get this part-time job at the Cooper Corrugated Box Company down on Spring Street. You know the place—the big building that looks like it's mad at somebody. Almost all warehouses have this personality. They all look mean and grumpy. Like they've eaten something that's gonna come up on 'em.

At Cooper's they fabricate paper, convert it into padding for shipping and boxes of all sizes. Maybe this is why the building looks the way it does, because of the stinking pulp. You should smell the joint. Kind of like a mixture of barf and rotten eggs.

At Cooper's, they've got corrugated paper products up the wazoo. Floor to ceiling bins of the crap. My job like is pulling orders for paper boxes. The boxes come broken down flat and are sold in bundles. My title is "Box Boy." Hey, how about this for a glamour I.D.? "Box Boy!" When I think of it, I get this image of a guy made out of a box.

I've been working at Cooper's for almost a year now. After school, on Saturdays, and during summer vacation. But I'm about to tell 'em to take their boxes and shove 'em sideways. The work is heavy, and I've got so many paper cuts my hands look like veal cutlets. Like I said, what if nobody did anything? Wouldn't we all be a helluva lot happier?